KAIO PUBLICATIONS, INC.

Visit www.kaiopublications.org
for more valuable resources.

Piedy is a character created by
the Piedmont Road Church of Christ.
His name is pronounced "Pee-dee."

Piedy Learns About Patience
Written and Created by Jake Sutton
Illustrated and Designed by Jeremy Pate
Edited by Tonja McRady
Published by Kaio Publications, Inc.
223 Town Center Pkwy #118, Spring Hill, TN 37174
ISBN: 978-1-952955-07-5

DEDICATIONS:

To Noah Brown, Reagan Bystedt, and Ty Spurlin - Thank you for being our AUTASTIC crew at Piedmont Road! We love you and your great families!—Jake Sutton

To anyone and everyone who has ever felt different. May you experience the love of Jesus through His people.—Jeremy Pate

Our Lord made it very clear while He was on this earth that the faith required in the kingdom of God is like that of a child's.

For God's glory—may this story help us all.

Since we last saw Piedy, some new families started coming to Piedmont Road to worship God.

One day after Bible study, everyone went to the playground to spend some time together.

While they were swinging on the swingset, Piedy and his pal, Roady, started talking about some of the new kids who had been visiting.

"Hey, Piedy," **said Roady,** "have you met those new girls yet?? One of them is kinda different. She chases butterflies and talks to herself. How silly is that?!"

"Roady, it's not nice to talk about people," **said Piedy.** "Have you even tried to get to *know* them yet?" **2**

"Psshh, no,"

Roady replied.

"They probably won't be here long anyway since they are so weird."

3

Piedy said,

"Well, I don't think that's very nice. And since we don't know them yet, I'm going over there to meet her!"

4

"Hi! I'm Piedy!" said Piedy to the new girl.

"I'm really glad that you got to come to Bible study today! Did you just move into town?"

The new girl didn't say anything.

"Hey, I love butterflies too!" **Piedy said.** "Aren't you glad that God created them?"

The new girl still didn't
answer, and began chasing
after the butterfly.

**The new girl's sister came
up to Piedy and said,**

"It's ok, pal.

I know that was a little strange, but
thank you for trying to be her friend!"

8

She told Piedy, "Her name is Patience, and I'm her twin sister Penelope! What's your name?"

"My name is Piedy," said Piedy. "So, why did she run away? Did I do something wrong?"

Penelope said, "Oh no, Piedy. You didn't do anything wrong. Patience is

AUTISTIC.

Sometimes her senses just can't handle everything going on around her."

"You mean like her five senses?" asked Piedy. "Hearing, tasting, seeing, touching, and smelling?

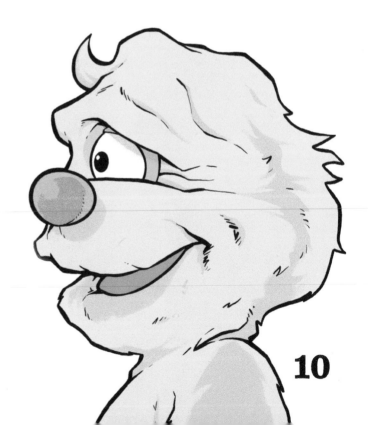

"Exactly, Piedy!" **answered Penelope.**
"Especially her *hearing*. Loud noises hurt
Patience's ears. That's why she covers
them up sometimes. It's because loud
noises make her uncomfortable."

11

Penelope continued, "For as long as I can remember, Patience has always been special.

There were times when she wouldn't play with me, and I didn't know why. That was really hard for me."

"And she didn't like it when I practiced my flute. She covered her ears, and that hurt my feelings."

"But after I learned that she couldn't help it, I understood, and I loved her even more!

I found out that she loves to read, especially about butterflies!

She also loves getting the mail. It's always a fun surprise for her to see what's in the mailbox!"

Piedy said, "I think I understand now. Thank you Penelope! I'll see you at worship on Sunday!"

14

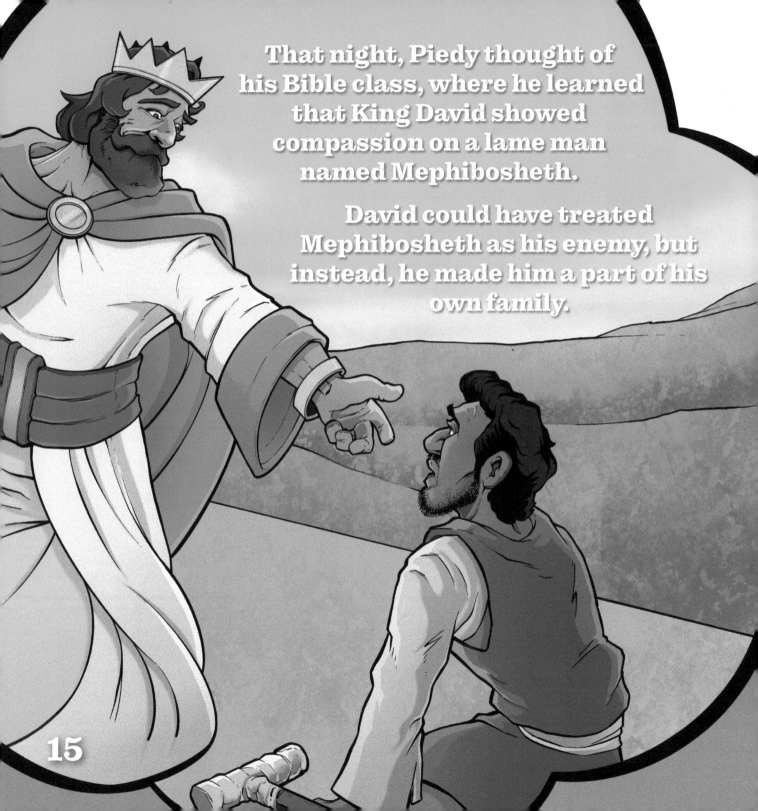

That night, Piedy thought of his Bible class, where he learned that King David showed compassion on a lame man named Mephibosheth.

David could have treated Mephibosheth as his enemy, but instead, he made him a part of his own family.

Like David (and Jesus), Piedy wanted to show kindness to Patience. So he wrote her a letter telling her how much God loves her, and that he would like for them to be pals. He also remembered that loud noises bothered Patience. Since he knew they would be singing loud in worship on Sunday, he also got her a special gift.

16

On Sunday morning, before worship started,
Piedy turned around in his seat to give
Patience her letter and her gift.

"Hi Patience!" he said. "I'm glad you came back
to worship today! I have a surprise for you!"

18

After reading Piedy's letter, Patience opened her gift and put on her headphones.

She was so happy, and she decided that she wanted to sit with Piedy during worship.

They all sang songs of worship
as loudly as they could.

As pals.

After worship, everyone went to the playground to play together. Roady said to Piedy,

"I saw what you did for Patience this morning, and I wanted to say I'm sorry. I really want to be pals with Patience."

"It's okay, Roady," **said Piedy.** "Everyone makes mistakes. I'm sure Patience will be your pal! She's awesome!"

"Did her sister help you understand why she chases butterflies?" **asked Roady.**

Piedy replied, "Yeah, and it's not because she is 'weird.' She's...'autastic.'"

"What does *that* mean?" **Roady asked. Piedy answered,** "Well, she's AUTISTIC *and* she's FANTASTIC, so, you know, she's...**AUTASTIC!!**"

22

How to draw Patience

On a separate sheet of paper, use these simple steps, practice drawing Patience! Remember, draw LIGHTLY until you get to the last step!

STEP ONE:

Start by drawing a circle, two curved lines, and the eyes and nose.

STEP TWO:

Using your circle/lines, add the fur, the lower jaw, and the mouth.

STEP THREE:

Add the hair bow and the shoulders.

STEP FOUR:

Draw Patience's eyelids, eyebrows, and pupils next.

STEP FIVE

Add some details to the face and mouth.

STEP SIX:

Finish your drawing by adding more fur and smile lines. Darken the lines you want to keep!

23

Autastic Word Search

Find the words listed below and circle them. The words can be found going up, down, and across.

```
H E A D P H O N E S O I
W B K Q G W R N M B S M
K L Q F Z A H O Z U I A
K P N L H K W T N T N I
I X T U L Q F Z Q T G L
N F O T U D W C S E I L
D M B E E L C J F R N O
N P A T I E N C E F G V
E Y L B O B M I Q L O E
S S Z G W G W K I Y P D
S D A V I D K W Y J M T
I F P E N E L O P E Q O
```

BUTTERFLY   **DAVID**   **FLUTE**
PATIENCE   **KINDNESS**   **MAIL**
PENELOPE   **HEADPHONES**   **LOVE**
                    SINGING

24

A Word About Autism:

Autism is a complex mental condition that is difficult (if not impossible) to adequately represent in a children's book. For those with autism—and for those who know and love them—everyone's experience is going to be different.

It is the goal of this book to give parents a "starting point" to talk to their children about autism, especially when it comes to how we should treat those who are different than we are. We believe this is concept that the Bible addresses, and one that Jesus taught and modeled.

For more information about autism, you can visit the following websites:

www.autismspeaks.com
www.autism-society.org
www.autismacceptance.org

25

MW00580334

CPSIA information can be obtained
at www.ICGtesting.com
Printed in the USA
BVHW020022130821
614291BV00021B/1165

9 781952 955075